THE NATIONAL TRUST
Little Library

Aromatic HERBS

JILL NORMAN

DORLING KINDERSLEY
LONDON

EDITOR GWEN EDMONDS

DESIGN MATHEWSON BULL

PHOTOGRAPHER DAVE KING

ART DIRECTOR STUART JACKMAN

FIRST PUBLISHED IN GREAT BRITAIN IN 1989 BY
DORLING KINDERSLEY LIMITED
9 HENRIETTA STREET, LONDON WC2E 8PS

BRITISH LIBRARY CATALOGUING IN PUBLICATION DATA

NORMAN, JILL
AROMATIC HERBS.
I. GARDENS. AROMATIC PLANTS
I. TITLE II. SERIES
635′.7

ISBN 0–86318–381–6

PRINTED AND BOUND IN HONG KONG
BY IMAGO

CONTENTS

INTRODUCTION

'Speak not – whisper not;
Here bloweth thyme and bergamot;
Softly on the evening hour,
Secret herbs their spices shower,
Dark-spiked rosemary and myrrh,
Lean-stalked, purple lavender;'

The Sunken Garden, *Walter de la Mare*

$\mathcal{E}$VERYONE CAN GROW HERBS, *whether in the garden, window boxes or containers. Most herbs prefer light well-drained soil and a sunny position. Sunlight develops their volatile oils which produce the plant's characteristic scent and flavour. The sweet smell of herbs in summer is one of the most agreeable things about growing them, and their flavours are readily transferred to a variety of dishes. Aromatic herbs are mostly used in cooked dishes and many may be used fresh or dried, though not necessarily interchangeably. You could not make a mint julep with dried mint, but dried mint is more successful than fresh in many dishes such as the Turkish kofte on page 35.*

These days a wide range of fresh herbs is available year round from many supermarkets if you don't grow your own. Some herbs keep well for a few days in a pot of water – coriander and parsley do particularly well; most keep up to a week in a loose plastic bag in the refrigerator and many, coriander, mint and horseradish among them, will freeze well if chopped and packed in small plastic pots, but frozen herbs should only be added to a dish for the last few minutes of its cooking time.

Parsley, basil and coriander do not dry well and dried tarragon has a less potent flavour than fresh. Mint, marjoram, oregano and rosemary do dry well and have a more concentrated flavour. So if you substitute dried for fresh herbs, do so sparingly. Dried herbs do not keep their aroma indefinitely – about a year is the maximum time, so only buy in small amounts.

To dry your own, gather the herbs on a dry day before the flowering time because the flavour is strongest then. Tie them in bundles and hang in a dark airy place or spread them on paper in a cupboard. It is not a good idea to dry them in a low oven unless forced to do so because of bad weather. Drying will take 10 to 20 days depend-ing on the

Commercial drying of herbs, c. 1923

plant and the conditions. Strip the leaves from the stalks and store in air-tight jars. It is useful to keep small quant-ities of dried herb mixtures too. Mrs Grieve recommends 'equal proportions of knotted marjoram and winter savory with half quant-ities of basil, thyme and tarragon, all rubbed to a powder' in Culinary Herbs and Condiments, 1934. Equal amounts of powdered rosemary, thyme, winter savory, bay leaves and grated lemon rind make a good seasoning for stuffing and stews, and for a fashionable Cajun flavour from Louisiana combine equal quantities of crushed thyme, oregano and basil with ground black and red chilli pepper and salt.

BASIL

*O*CIMUM BASILICUM, *is a tropical member of the mint family, with a spicy flavour and scent. Best used fresh but will keep in a jar with olive oil and a little salt. Asian varieties, used sparingly in India but abundantly in Thai cooking, are more pungent than those from cooler climates.*

Ocimum basilicum

Fresh basil goes well with tomatoes, raw or cooked. Aubergine and pepper dishes benefit from basil, as does a good firm fish such as mullet or sea bass. Combined with garlic it gives a peppery flavour to plain chicken dishes and, as pesto, makes the ultimate pasta sauce. Basil vinegar brightens many a winter salad.

BAY

*T*HE TOUGH LEAVES *of the laurel tree* (Laurus nobilis), *and in India the mellower ones of the cassia tree, are used fresh or dried to impart a spicy aroma to many different dishes. In medieval Europe bay was a popular strewing herb, for its scent and antiseptic properties. In Moghul pilafs it is one of the four essential spices.*

Bay leaves are basic to much Mediterranean and French cooking, in marinades and pickles, court bouillon, bouquet garni, stews and the milk used for cream sauces.

The fresh leaves can often be a little bitter, but the bitterness (unlike the scent) fades quickly. Leaves should be dried in the dark to retain their colour.

Laurus nobilis

7

BERGAMOT

*M*ONARDA DIDYMA, *also called Bee balm, is a North American member of the mint family. As 'Oswego tea' (from its Indian origin) it became popular in the New World after the Boston Tea Party of 1773 and, not much later, even in England. Fresh, it adds spice to fruit cups.*

Bergamot must be used sparingly but is good in salads (both leaves and bright flowers) or stuffings and to flavour jams, jellies and the milk used for puddings.

The whole plant gives off a pleasant lemony fragrance and for this reason has long been a favourite in garden borders. Its culinary use has on the whole been sadly neglected.

Monarda didyma

CORIANDER

*A*LTHOUGH CORIANDER (CORIANDRUM SATIVUM) *has been well known in China and India for thousands of years, it was Arab cooking that spread the use of both the herb and its small seed through the Middle East, North Africa, Spain and Portugal and from there to the New World.*

Known as 'Chinese parsley' but called 'the fragrant plant' in China itself, where it is much used chopped up fine in sauces. In India the seed is essential; from the Middle East westward herb and seed are equal partners. The herb is normally used fresh. It does not dry, but freezes well or can be kept, like basil, preserved with salt in oil. It does not take well to long cooking, and it is therefore best added at a late stage. India and South America use the excellent combination of coriander and green chillies in chutneys and sauces. Soups, salads and stuffings benefit greatly from it. Thai cuisine uses the roots to flavour stews.

Coriandrum sativum

GARLIC

*A*LLIUM SATIVUM *is a staple of everyday cooking for all but the Anglo-Saxons. A tonic and a seasoning, with great warming qualities, it balances sharper flavours such as ginger or chilli. Make sure you buy hard cloves that are free of spots.*

Raw garlic has a strong taste; cooked it is mild and leaves no trace on the breath. When frying, remove garlic before it browns.

Allium sativum

The basis of **strong sauces** such as aïoli and rouille, and the more subtle flavouring in many meat, game and fish recipes, it blends well with many vegetables and with most herbs and spices. Slow-cooked heads make a mellow accompaniment to roasts.

HORSERADISH

*A*RMORACIA RUSTICANA *is easily recognisable by its large crinkly leaves which grow, palm-like, straight up from the root, or in summer by its white flowers on their long spike. It is not easy to dig up as it develops a rather complex root system – and it is the roots that are used.*

Scrubbed (or, if you want pure white horseradish, peeled) and grated – a process more eye watering than onion peeling – it may be used instantly, but its active life can be prolonged by making a sauce with yoghurt or cream and some sugar and vinegar, or blending to a staple condiment with dry mustard, water, salt and pepper.

Armoracia rusticana

11

LOVAGE

L EVISTICUM OFFICINALE *is a rather neglected herb that was popular in classical Greece and Rome. Its wild form, growing along Atlantic coasts, was used as a vegetable in Scotland and America. The stems can be candied; the seeds give a taste of celery to wholemeal bread.*

A few fresh leaves will liven up a green salad and, shredded, go well with tomato and egg dishes. Try lovage butter with potatoes.

Lovage is a good addition to vegetable dishes. Its yeasty flavour gives an almost meaty taste, notably to pulses but also to stuffings or sauces. It makes excellent soup by itself or can be used to flavour other soups.

Levisticum officinale

PARSLEY

*P*ETROSELINUM CRISPUM *has become the standard decora-tive herb of the Anglo-Saxon world, whilst European cooking adds parsley almost as easily as salt, often as a last-minute 'persillade' (with shallots) or 'picada' (with nuts and garlic).*

Parsley is always used fresh. The stalks are an essential ingredient of bouquet garni, as the finely chopped leaves are of many sauces (often together with lemon or lemon balm) and a number of butters, including maître d'hôtel and garlic butter.

Indonesian cooking uses parsley (introduced by the Dutch) and in Turkey parsley omelettes herald the coming of spring. Parsley is decorative in aspic or deep-fried.

Petroselinum crispum

Petroselinum sativum

MARJORAM & OREGANO

*M*ARJORAM (ORIGANUM MAJORANA) *has been cultivated for its medicinal and culinary properties for many centuries in the Middle East. Introduced into Europe in medieval times its fragrance was valued for toilet waters. Today its use is confined to the kitchen where often it is interchangeable with thyme. Sweet marjoram is not as hardy as the coarser pot marjoram.*

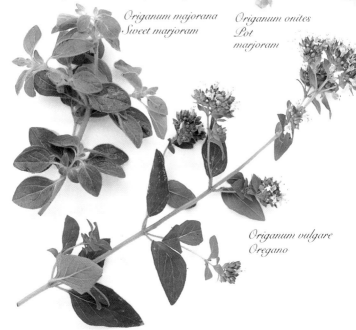

Origanum majorana
Sweet marjoram

Origanum onites
Pot
marjoram

Origanum vulgare
Oregano

Oregano (*O. vulgare*) is the common name for wild marjoram which grows from the Himalayas to the British Isles – and in Mexico for unrelated plants with the same properties. In warm climates the herb is much more pungent and peppery than in cool wet ones. Both marjoram and oregano can be used when dried. In fact, the latter is not normally exported in any other form since it retains a remarkably concentrated flavour. The delicate flavour of sweet marjoram is easily lost in cooking: add it only towards the end. The fresh herb, chopped, with some lemon juice, makes a good dressing. Oregano provides the pungent flavouring of pizza. It goes particularly well with onion, aubergine, tomato, beans and meat.

O.v. aureum
Golden marjoram

O.v. Pink flowered marjoram

MINT

MINT (MENTHA SPECIES) *has been used as a flavouring herb since antiquity. From its native Mediterranean habitat it spread throughout Europe with the Roman legions. Many mints are cultivated or grow wild; the best for flavour is spearmint. Apple and Bowles' mints with their woolly-looking leaves are also popular in the kitchen. Peppermint makes a flavouring oil for sweets.*

Mentha spicata
Spearmint

Mentha spicata variegata
Variegated apple mint

Mint does not blend easily with other herbs, but its potent and refreshing flavour suits a wide range of other ingredients: the new potatoes and marrow-fat peas of England; dishes of mutton and lamb; the yoghurt and cucumber salad of Turkey and the Balkans; sweet teas of India and Morocco or the equally sweet whisky-based mint julep of North America. Mint is the main herb in Moghul cooking, it is widely used in India and the Middle East. It dries well, retaining its great strength.

M. × *villosa*
Bowles' mint

ROSEMARY

*A*NOTHER HERB *of Mediterranean origin,* Rosmarinus officinalis *grows well in other parts of Europe and in North America. It is an aromatic plant which thrives in any warm dry place, even with the poorest soil. Its leathery and spiky leaves have a strong flavour with a hint of pine needles but also of the camphor which is part of its essential oil. Rosemary, which has very pretty pale blue flowers during a long season, is an evergreen bush so the herb is always available fresh.*

Rosmarinus officinalis

Rosemary is normally used whole, in sprigs, for the hard leaves are not very pleasant and their taste, when chewed, is a little overpowering. It blends well with garlic and wine in marinades or cooking liquids for rabbit and other small game. Its traditional use is in roasting or grilling, mostly lamb or kid, but also fish and shellfish, especially over a barbecue.

SAGE

*T*HE MANY VARIETIES OF **Salvia officinalis** include both decorative and culinary plants. Among the latter, the blue-flowered and narrow-leaved variety and the usually non-flowering broad-leaved ones are those commonly used. Names such as pineapple, lavender or wormwood sage hint at the differences in flavour.

Salvia officinalis

Sage shares with rosemary the reputation of being somewhat crude (camphor is the culprit again) but its usefulness goes beyond sage and onion stuffing to interesting dishes of eel, ham, liver, sausages and veal, as well as flavouring for beans or peas and kebabs.

SAVORY

*T*HE ROMANS *brought savory* (Satureja montana) *from the Mediterranean to the rest of Europe, and later migrants took it to the New World. Summer and winter savory are but two of a number of species which were commonly used until the arrival of the stronger spices from the East. The spiky leaves are best before the flowering.*

The rather aggressive, peppery flavour of savory (which the dried herb retains) is traditionally used in sausages, stuffings, and with both fresh and dried beans. It goes well with cucumber, and blended with other herbs makes a good seasoning for fish.

Satureja montana

TARRAGON

*A*RTEMISIA DRACUNCULUS' *tangy and slightly bitter taste betrays its relation to wormwood. From its Middle Eastern origins it reached Europe only in the 16th century, via Moorish Spain. It is a herb with a variety of uses, from providing an appetizing scent on a barbecue fire to being frozen in ice cubes to flavour cold drinks.*

French tarragon has a more subtle aroma and flavour than the Russian (*A. dracunculoides*). It can be used in roasting, or as tarragon butter with asparagus or artichokes.

Artemisia dracunculus

Tarragon vinegar, made by steeping the fresh herb in white wine vinegar for two months, is a fine kitchen staple for salad dressings, mustards and many sauces.

THYME

*T*HE THYMUS SPECIES *was named by the ancient Greeks, but probably even they were not the first to exploit its culinary properties. Many species, with varying flavours, grow wild in the hot and dry parts of western Asia, North Africa and southern Europe; others have been cultivated for cooler climates.*

*Thymus pulegioides
Broad leaf thyme*

Thyme is an essential herb in most Western cooking. It is a standard component of bouquet garni and many a court bouillon, goes well with vegetables (from tomato to potato) and with fish or in stuffings. It withstands slow cooking in stews, where it blends easily with garlic, onion and brandy or red wine to give a deep aroma. It gives similar qualities to marinades for pork and large game, and even to a pickle for olives.

*Thymus
p. a. 'Aureus'
Golden creeping thyme*

*T. × citriodorus
argenteus
Silver lemon thyme*

Thyme dries quite well, but the more delicate components of its complex flavour seem to be subdued in the process. Several species are grown for decorative use (silver leaf, golden creeper) while others such as lemon thyme are valuable kitchen variants.

Thymus vulgaris
Common thyme

*Thymus
serpyllum*
Wild thyme

T. × citriodorus
Lemon thyme

Recipes

*The recipes will serve 4,
but some (such as breads)
will serve more*

HERB BREAD

I like rosemary to flavour this
bread but sage, thyme or
marjoram work well too.

6 fl oz/175 ml milk
1 teaspoon salt
½ oz/15 g butter
½ packet easy blend dried yeast or
¼ oz/7 g ordinary dried yeast
12 oz/375 g strong white flour
6 fl oz/175 ml warm water
2 tablespoons finely chopped
fresh rosemary or 2 teaspoons dried

Heat the milk and stir in the salt
and butter until dissolved.
Sprinkle the easy blend yeast
over the flour, or if you are
using ordinary dried yeast leave
to prove in the warm water. Stir
the water into the flour, then the
milk. Scatter over the rosemary
and stir until well blended. The
dough should be quite soft and

batter-like and it is easily mixed with a wooden spoon. Cover and leave to rise in a warm place until at least doubled in bulk – about 1 hour.

Stir and beat thoroughly for a minute or so, then pour the batter into a greased 8 in/20 cm loaf tin and bake at once in a preheated oven – 180°C, 350°F, gas 4 for about 1 hour. When it is done the bottom should sound hollow when tapped.

Cool on a rack

This bread will keep for a day or so, but it is much better fresh.

FOCCACIA WITH SAGE

½ packet easy blend dried yeast or
¼ oz/7 g ordinary dried yeast
12 oz/375 g strong white flour
8 fl oz/250 ml warm water
1 teaspoon salt
2 tablespoons chopped fresh sage
leaves or 2 teaspoons dried
olive oil

Sprinkle the easy blend yeast over the flour or leave ordinary dried yeast to prove in the warm water. Mix the salt and sage into the flour. Add 1 tablespoon oil and the water and mix to a soft dough. Knead on a floured surface, or in the bowl until you have a springy, elastic dough. Oil the bowl lightly and leave the dough to rise for about 50 minutes or until it has doubled in bulk. On a floured surface, roll out the dough to a circle 1 in/2.5 cm thick. Put the foccacia on a greased baking sheet; make some indentations in the surface with your fingers and leave to rise for 30 minutes. Brush with olive oil, sprinkle with coarse salt and bake in a preheated oven – 190°C, 375°F, gas 5 for about 40 minutes. Foccacia is best eaten the day it is made.

Bouquet Garni

*A few sprigs of thyme, a bay leaf
and 2 or 3 fresh parsley stalks*
make up a standard bouquet
garni, but a stalk of celery, a
sprig of another herb such as
lovage, marjoram or savory may
be added. In Provence a strip of
orange peel is common; for a
fish dish a strip of lemon peel
would be appropriate. The
herbs are tied in a bundle so
they can be removed at the end
of the cooking time.

Tomato Sauce

*1 small onion, chopped finely
2 tablespoons olive oil
2 cloves garlic, crushed
1 lb/500 g tomatoes, chopped
2 tablespoons tomato paste
1 sprig thyme
1 bay leaf
2 tablespoons chopped parsley
1/4 pint/150 ml white wine
3 tablespoons water
salt and pepper*

Sauté the onion in oil until soft.
Add the garlic and continue to
cook, then 2 minutes later stir in
the tomatoes, tomato paste,
thyme, bay leaf and parsley.
Season with salt and pepper,
then pour in the
wine and water.
Stir thoroughly,
cover and simmer
for 20 minutes.
Sieve the sauce
and serve.

BASIL, MINT AND RED PEPPER SAUCE

a large handful of basil leaves
3–4 sprigs mint
1 sweet red pepper
3 tablespoons olive oil
2 tablespoons red wine vinegar
1 small clove garlic, chopped finely
salt and pepper

Strip the leaves from the mint sprigs and chop them finely with the basil leaves. Scorch the pepper over a gas flame or under a grill until it is blackened all over, then wrap in damp kitchen paper for a few minutes. The skin will then rub off easily. Remove the seeds and membranes and chop the flesh finely. Mix together the oil, vinegar, garlic and seasonings. Stir in the herbs and pepper. The sauce goes particularly well with cold fish, such as poached skate or turbot.

HORSERADISH, APPLE AND BEETROOT SALAD

2 oz/50 g horseradish, grated
3 tablespoons wine vinegar
1 tablespoon sugar
2 firm eating apples
3 tablespoons olive oil
8 oz/250 g cooked beetroot, cubed
fresh black pepper

Mix the horseradish, 2 tablespoons vinegar and the sugar together. Peel, quarter and slice the apples and mix with the horseradish. Add 2 tablespoons oil and blend thoroughly.

Toss the beetroot in the remaining oil and vinegar, season with black pepper. Pile it in the centre of a dish and surround with the apple and horseradish.

CARROT SALAD

Dress *grated carrot* with *olive oil* and *lemon juice*. Season with *salt* and *pepper* and finely chopped *lovage* or *coriander*. Toss and leave for half an hour for the flavours to blend.

PERSIAN CHICK PEA SOUP WITH MEAT BALLS

6 oz/175 g lean beef, minced
1 onion, finely chopped
¼ teaspoon cinnamon
salt and pepper
6 oz/175 g chick peas, soaked
overnight
4 oz/125 g lentils
2 leeks, sliced thinly
6 oz/175 g spinach, chopped
6 oz/175 g assorted fresh herbs –
lovage, mint, parsley, coriander,
dill, chopped
1 oz/25 g butter

Mix together thoroughly the meat, onion, cinnamon with salt and pepper to taste and make meatballs, the size of a walnut. Set them aside.
Put the chick peas in a large pan with 2½ pints/1.5 litres water, bring to the boil, then cover and simmer for 30 minutes. Add the meatballs and lentils and continue to cook for 30 minutes more. Then put in the leeks and spinach, simmer for another 20 minutes, add the herbs and cook for 10 minutes. Remove from the heat, stir in the butter and serve.

LOVAGE SOUP

1 oz/25 g butter
1 onion, chopped
2 tablespoons flour
1 pint/600 ml chicken stock
3 tablespoons chopped lovage leaves
juice ½ lemon
salt and pepper
¼ pint/150 ml single cream

Melt the butter, cook the onion until soft, then add the flour and stir well. Pour on the stock, a little at a time, and stir until the soup has thickened somewhat. Add the lovage and lemon juice and simmer for 20 minutes. Season with salt and pepper, then purée in a blender or through a sieve. Stir in the cream, heat through gently and serve.

FISH SOUP WITH TARRAGON

1 large onion, sliced
white part of 2 leeks, sliced
1 large potato, diced
1 bay leaf
2 sprigs tarragon
salt, white pepper
12 oz/375 g white fish fillets
¼ pint/150 ml single cream
1 tablespoon chopped fresh tarragon

Put the vegetables in a pan with the bay leaf, tarragon sprigs and 1 pint/600 ml water. Season with salt and pepper, bring to the boil and simmer, covered, for 10 minutes. Add the fish, cut in large pieces, and simmer until it will flake easily – about 8-10 minutes. Lift out the fish pieces and flake. Remove the bay leaf and tarragon sprigs. Stir the cream into soup and heat gently. Return the fish to the soup, heat through and serve sprinkled with chopped tarragon.

MUSSEL SALAD

2 lb/1kg mussels
2 onions
3 carrots
2 leeks
3 stalks celery
6 oz/175 g celeriac
2 cloves garlic
4 tablespoons olive oil
a large bunch of parsley
3 tomatoes, peeled and seeded
salt and pepper
lemon juice

Scrub the mussels and remove the beards, discarding any that are broken or open. Put them in a heavy pan over medium heat, cover with a lid and leave for 5 minutes or so until they open. Strain into a bowl, reserving the liquor.

Dice or chop all the vegetables finely. Chop the garlic and parsley. Soften the onion in the oil, then add the leeks, carrots, celery, celeriac and garlic. Cook for a few minutes, stirring to coat them with oil. Strain the mussel liquor twice through a muslin cloth and add about ¼ pint/150 ml to the vegetables. Cover and simmer gently until the vegetables are cooked. If necessary add a little more liquid. Remove the mussels from their shells, discarding any that haven't opened. Add the mussels and parsley to the vegetables and cook uncovered for 10 minutes so that the liquid reduces somewhat. Add the tomatoes, taste and season if necessary with salt and pepper. Turn into a serving dish, squeeze over a little lemon juice and leave to cool.

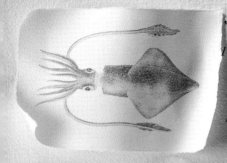

COD STEAKS WITH PARSLEY AND LEMON THYME

4 cod steaks
6 tablespoons dry breadcrumbs
4 tablespoons chopped parsley
2 tablespoons chopped lemon thyme
salt and pepper
2 tablespoons olive oil

Combine the breadcrumbs and herbs. Season the fish on both sides and brush with oil. Press some of the herb mixture firmly onto both sides of the steaks and drizzle more oil over them. Put the fish in a lightly oiled baking dish and cook for 8 minutes in a preheated oven, 200°C, 400°F, gas 6. Finish the fish briefly under the grill to turn the coating crusty.
Serve with tomato sauce (p. 26).

STUFFED SQUID

4 medium squid
1 oz/25 g dried mushrooms
1 small onion, chopped
2 tablespoons oil
3 oz/75 g rice, parboiled
1 teaspoon dried thyme
1 teaspoon dried oregano
grated rind of 2 lemons
salt and pepper
tomato sauce (p. 26)

Clean the squid, remove the pink filmy skin, the wings and the innards and head. Rinse the sacks well; cut the tentacles from the heads and chop finely with the wings.
Soak the mushrooms in hot water for 30 minutes. Heat the oil and fry the onion and chopped squid for 5 minutes over low heat. Add the drained rice, herbs and lemon rind. Drain the mushrooms, chop and add to the pan. Season well. Fill the squid pouches three quarters full and sew up the ends or fasten them with toothpicks. Cook the squid slowly in the tomato sauce for 30-40 minutes. Do not let them cook too quickly or the squid will be tough.

STIR-FRIED THAI CHICKEN

3-4 chicken breasts, skinned and boned
1 tablespoon cornflour
2 tablespoons brandy or sherry
2 tablespoons soy sauce
2 fresh red chillies, seeded and chopped
1 tablespoon rice vinegar
1 tablespoon sugar
½ teaspoon powdered lemon grass
2 tablespoons oil
1 onion, sliced thinly
a handful of basil leaves, chopped
a handful of mint leaves, chopped
1 lime, cut in wedges

Cut the chicken into cubes.
Whisk together the cornflour,
brandy, and 1 tablespoon soy
sauce and marinate the chicken
for 15 minutes. Combine the
remaining soy sauce with the
chillies, vinegar, sugar and
lemon grass and set aside.
Heat the oil in a wok and stir-fry
the onion and chicken for 2-3
minutes until the onions are soft
and the chicken starts to colour.
Add the soy mixture and half
the basil and mint. Continue
stirring and turning for a minute
or two until the chicken is tender.
Transfer to a warm serving dish.
Scatter the remaining herbs
over the chicken and serve with
the wedges of lime.

ℛOAST PORK WITH SAGE

2 lb/1 kg pork loin, bones and skin removed, and rolled
10 sage leaves
1 clove garlic, cut in slivers
large sprig thyme
1 bay leaf
salt
2 tablespoons olive oil

With the point of a sharp knife pierce the meat on all sides and insert the sage leaves and garlic slivers. Strip the leaves from the thyme and mix with the crumbled bay leaf and salt. Rub the meat with this mixture and put it into a small roasting tin. Pour over the oil and roast in a preheated oven, 180°C, 350°F, gas 4 for 1 hour, basting occasionally. Leave the meat to rest for 10 minutes in a warm place before carving.
The pork is also good cold with a potato salad.

ℛABBIT WITH ROSEMARY

4 pieces rabbit
¼ pint/150 ml olive oil
1 clove garlic, crushed
2-3 sprigs rosemary
juice ½ lemon
¼ pint/150 ml white wine
2 tomatoes, peeled, seeded and chopped
salt and pepper
2 oz/50 g small black olives

Marinate the rabbit in the oil, garlic, rosemary and lemon juice for 6 to 8 hours, turning occasionally. Transfer the rabbit and the marinade to a heavy pan and cook over a low heat for 20 minutes. Add the wine, bring to the boil and reduce slightly, then add the tomatoes, season with salt and pepper and simmer for a further 25 minutes. Put in the olives and cook for another 5 minutes. Remove the rosemary sprigs and serve.

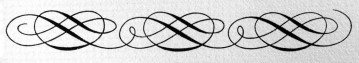

Bœuf en Daube

2 lb/1 kg topside of beef
2 onions, quartered
2 carrots, sliced
2 bouquets garnis
1/2 pint/300 ml red wine
oil
4 oz/125 g salt pork
4 cloves garlic, crushed
strip of orange peel
pinch cayenne
salt and pepper

Cut the beef into 8-10 pieces and put it in a bowl with the onion, carrot, a bouquet garni, salt, wine and 1 tablespoon oil and marinate for 4-5 hours or longer, turning the meat occasionally.

Remove the rind from the salt pork and cut it into thin strips. Cut the salt pork in small cubes. Put another tablespoon of oil into an earthenware casserole, put in the salt pork and rinds, the drained meat and vegetables. Place the garlic cloves among the contents, put a new bouquet garni and a strip of orange peel in the middle of the casserole and season with pepper and a little cayenne.

Pour over the marinade liquor. Bring slowly to the boil on the top of the stove, uncovered, and let the wine reduce a little. Add 1/4 pint/150 ml water. Cover the casserole with a layer of foil and a tight fitting lid. Cook in a preheated oven – 150°C, 300°F, gas 2 for 3½-4 hours.

Skim off some of the fat and remove the bouquet and orange peel before serving.

LOVAGE AND POTATO OMELETTE

This is a substantial omelette, like a Spanish tortilla.

4 tablespoons olive oil
1 medium onion, chopped
4 oz/125 g bacon or cured ham, diced
3 medium potatoes, cooked and diced
4 eggs
a handful of lovage leaves, chopped
salt and pepper

Heat 2 tablespoons oil in a large frying pan and sauté the onion until golden. Add the bacon and potatoes and cook for 4-5 minutes more. Beat the eggs lightly in a bowl, season to taste, then mix in the vegetables and bacon and the lovage.

Clean the pan well, heat the remaining oil until hot and pour in the egg mixture. Cook over low heat, shaking the pan to prevent sticking. When the eggs are set put a plate over the pan and turn the omelette upside down onto it. Add a little more oil if necessary, then slide the omelette back into the pan to cook for a few minutes longer.

Serve hot or at room temperature, cut in wedges.

TURKISH KOFTE

These kofte can be moulded into a sausage shape round a skewer or shaped like hamburgers.

1 lb/500 g minced lamb
1 small onion, chopped finely
2 teaspoons dried mint
1/2 teaspoon red pepper flakes
salt

Combine all the ingredients and work to a paste in a food processor. Divide in four and work with wet hands to the shape you wish. Cook under a grill or on a barbecue for 8-10 minutes.

RICE WITH MINT AND CORIANDER

8 oz/250 g Basmati rice
a handful of coriander leaves
a handful of mint leaves
2 green chillies
1 onion
3 fl oz/75 ml oil
4 cloves
2 in/5 cm stick cinnamon
1 teaspoon salt

Wash the rice well and leave to soak in clean water for 30 minutes. Chop the herbs finely; remove the seeds and chop the chillies; chop the onion finely. Heat the oil in a large pan until very hot, add the cloves and cinnamon, then the rice, and stir well to coat all the grains with oil. Add the herbs, chilli, onion and salt, pour over 1 pint/600 ml cold water, stir briefly and bring to the boil. Reduce the heat and simmer, covered, for 15 minutes or until most of the water is absorbed and there are holes on the surface. Turn off the heat but leave the tightly covered pan on the hot surface for another 15 minutes. Stir with a fork to avoid breaking the grains, turn out onto a warm dish and serve.

ROASTED GARLIC

Roasted garlic is best made with new garlic in the summer. It has a mellow flavour that goes well with roast lamb or chicken.

4 heads garlic
2 tablespoons olive oil
salt and pepper

Separate the garlic heads into cloves, but don't peel them. Put them into an earthenware baking dish, pour over the oil, making sure all the cloves are coated. Add salt and pepper to taste and roast in a preheated oven, 180°C, 350°F, gas 4 for 20-30 minutes, basting from time to time. When done the soft flesh slips out of the skin quite easily.

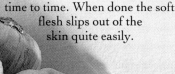

TIAN OF TOMATOES AND AUBERGINES

2 large aubergines
1 onion, chopped
olive oil
2 cloves garlic, chopped finely
a handful of basil leaves
2 eggs
salt and pepper
3 large tomatoes
2 tablespoons breadcrumbs
2 tablespoons grated parmesan

Cube the aubergines and cook in boiling salted water for 5 minutes. Drain and put aside. Cook the onion in 1 tablespoon oil for 10 minutes until soft, then add the garlic. Tear the basil leaves into small pieces. Beat the eggs, season with salt and pepper and stir in the aubergine, onion, garlic and half the basil. Brush a gratin dish with a little oil and pour in the mixture. Sprinkle with oil, slice the tomatoes and arrange them on top. Season with salt and pepper and scatter with the remaining basil. Spread the breadcrumbs and parmesan over everything and add a little more oil. Bake in a preheated oven, 190°C, 375°F, gas 5 for 35 minutes.

BRAISED ARTICHOKES

4 artichokes
a small bunch of parsley, chopped
1 teaspoon mixed herbs –
marjoram, savory, thyme
1 bay leaf
4 cloves garlic
¼ pint/150 ml olive oil
8 fl oz/250 ml white wine
salt and black pepper

Break off the stalks, remove the
tough outer leaves and trim the
tops of the artichokes. Put them,
the right way up, in a heavy pan
in which they just fit. Scatter the
herbs and garlic among them.
Pour over the oil, wine, and add
just enough water to cover.
Season, cover the pan and bring
to the boil, then simmer for 30-
40 minutes. When a leaf pulls out
easily the artichokes are ready.
Serve with the cooking liquid,
reduced by boiling if necessary,
as a sauce.

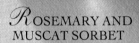

𝓜INT JULEP

For each person put *a teaspoon of caster sugar* and *2 teaspoons of water* into a tall glass and stir to dissolve the sugar. Add *3–4 sprigs of mint*, fill the glass with crushed ice and pour over a large measure of *Bourbon whiskey*. Put a couple more sprigs of mint on top and serve with a straw.

𝓑ERGAMOT AND LEMON SORBET

8 oz/250 g sugar
1/2 pint/300 ml water
6 sprigs bergamot
1 egg white
1/4 pint/150 ml lemon juice

Make a syrup by dissolving the sugar in the water and then boiling hard for 3 minutes. Infuse the bergamot in the syrup and leave until cold. Strain. Whisk the egg white lightly and add to the syrup with the lemon juice. Pour into an ice cream machine and freeze according to the manufacturer's instructions.

𝓡OSEMARY AND MUSCAT SORBET

1/2 pint/300 ml water
4 oz/125 g sugar
3–4 sprigs rosemary
1 egg white
8 fl oz/250 ml muscat

For a rich, sweet muscat flavour use a wine such as Beaumes-de-Venise; for a lighter dryer muscat taste use a muscat from Alsace. Bring the water and sugar to the boil and boil hard for 3 minutes. Infuse the rosemary in the syrup and leave until cold, then strain. Whisk the egg white lightly and add to the syrup. Stir in the wine, pour into an ice cream machine and freeze according to the manufacturer's instructions.

INDEX

ACKNOWLEDGEMENTS

Dorling Kindersley
would like to thank the
following people:

JACKET
· PHOTOGRAPHY ·
DAVE KING

· TYPESETTING ·
WYVERN
TYPESETTING LTD

· ILLUSTRATORS ·
JANE THOMSON
SHEILAGH NOBLE

FALKINER FINE
PAPERS LTD

· REPRODUCTION ·
COLOURSCAN
SINGAPORE